SUPER SPORTS

Air Sports

DAVID JEFFERIS

RAINTREE
STECK-VAUGHN
RSVP PUBLISHERS

A Harcourt Company

Austin   New York
www.raintreesteckvaughn.com

Published by Raintree Steck-Vaughn Publishers, an imprint of Steck-Vaughn Company

Library of Congress Cataloging-in-Publication Data

Jefferis, David.
    Air sports / David Jefferis.
        p. cm. -- (Super sports)
    Includes bibliographical references and index.
        ISBN 0-7398-4343-5
        1. Aeronautical sports--Juvenile literature.
[1. Aeronautical sports] I. Title. II. Super sports (Austin, Tex.)

GV755 .J44 2001
797.5--dc21   2001017051

Acknowledgments
We wish to thank the following individuals and organizations for their help and assistance and for supplying material in their collections:
Action-Plus Photographic, AllSport UK Ltd, Alpha Archive, Steve Crampton, D. Cubbitt, Jon Davison, John M. Dibbs/ The Plane Picture Company, Paul Harrison, Mike Hewitt, Didier Klein, Genevieve Leaper, Peter R. March, Leo Mason, Michael O'Leary, Ian Pillinger, Andy Richardson, François Rickard, Skyscan Photolibrary, Vandystadt Sports Photos, Keith Wilson, David Wootton

Diagrams by Gavin Page

Printed in China and bound in the United States.

1 2 3 4 5 6 7 05 04 03 02 01

▲ Sky divers leap from a helicopter. In seconds they will be falling at almost 124 miles (200 km) per hour. When their parachutes are released, each sky diver should slow down and be able to land as gently as a feather.

Contents

Look out for the Super Sports symbol
Look for the aircraft symbol in boxes like this.
Here you will find extra air sports facts, stories,
and useful tips for beginners.

◀ This first-time sky diver falls with an instructor. The parachute is big enough for two.

World of Air Sports

The thrill of flying high above the earth is the appeal of air sports. But good training and knowing safe ways of doing things is very important.

Air sports fall in two main groups—with power and without power. Gliding is a good air sport without power. In most countries, you can glide before you are allowed to drive!

▼ Gliders can stay up for hours. The rising currents of air support them.

4

▲ A paraglider has a nylon wing. This one is a two-seater.

Other air sports include skydiving and paragliding. A paraglider looks like a parachute, but it is flown like a glider.
    Aircraft with power range from tiny one-seaters to high-speed jets.

▶ Aerobatic teams are a thrill to watch at air shows.

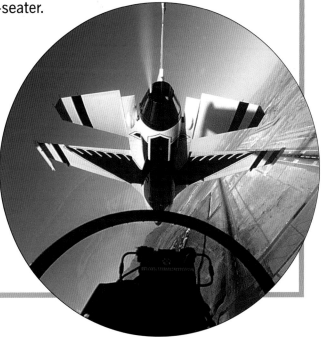

Lighter Than Air

The first people to fly, in the eighteenth century, used hot-air balloons. Today, hot-air balloons that run on gas are popular.

◀ The best time to launch a balloon is early morning or evening, when the air is calmer than during the day.

People ride in a square basket under the balloon.

Hot-air balloons rise because hot air is lighter than cool air. A gas burner sends a jet of flame into the balloon's neck to warm the air inside. For takeoff, the pilot turns the burner control up. Then with a loud roar, flames leap into the balloon to heat the air inside even more.

The balloon starts to lift, while ground crews hang on to lines attached to the basket. Then the pilot calls, "Let go," and the balloon rises into the sky.

6

Stand by for takeoff!

It takes some time to make a hot-air balloon ready to fly. The air has to be very calm, since even slight gusts can blow a balloon sideways. The air inside can weigh a ton or more. That is a lot for ground crew to control.

The first step is to unload the equipment from its trailer.

1 The balloon is left in the bag while the pilot checks that the gas burner works well.

2 The balloon is unrolled and spread out. Lines attach it to the wicker basket.

3 A powerful cold-air fan is used to blow air into the balloon to give it some shape.

4 The pilot shoots jets of fire inside. The air warms up, and the balloon starts to rise.

5 The balloon sways overhead as the pilot makes checks before flight. If there is a fault, now is the time to fix it.

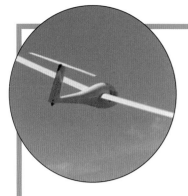

Soaring in the Sky

▲ Gliders have a very smooth shape, so that they can slip through the air easily.

Gliding is a challenge. Glider pilots need to be skillful to stay in the air. On a good day, a pilot can fly high in the sky.

To start gliding, the glider needs a lift from a tow plane or a winch-launch. (See page 29.) A long cable is attached under the glider's nose, and then the glider is pulled into the sky. At about 1,970-2,300 feet (600-700 m), the tow-cable is released, and the glider is on its own.

Beginners start by learning to steer and make a smooth landing. The next step is learning to spot rising air and using it to fly higher and longer. Expert pilots can cover long distances and stay up for hours at a time.

Three kinds of lift

Gliders need rising air, or lift, to stay up. There are three kinds of lift.

Thermals are bubbles of warm air heated by the sun. Pilots fly in tight circles to stay in a thermal and rise up with it.

Ridge lift is created when air blows up the side of a hill.

Wave lift is when air blows over the top of a hill, goes down the other side, then "bounces" upward.

▶ On hot, sunny days glider pilots have to protect their heads with sunhats!

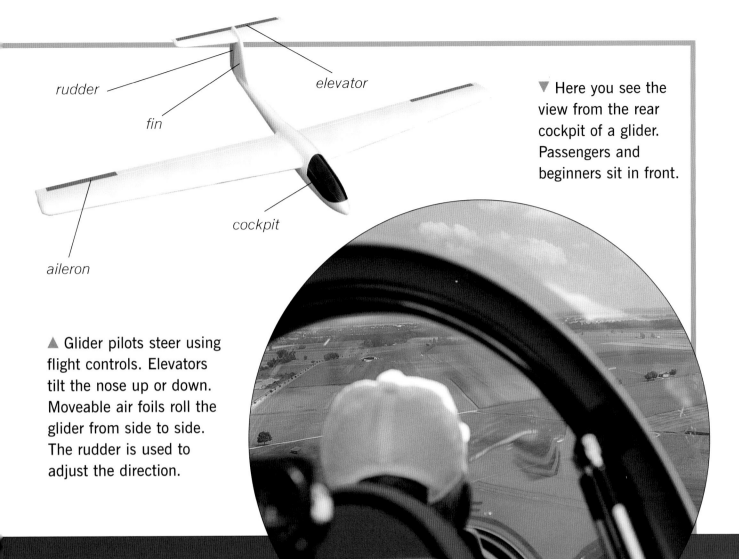

rudder

elevator

fin

cockpit

aileron

▼ Here you see the view from the rear cockpit of a glider. Passengers and beginners sit in front.

▲ Glider pilots steer using flight controls. Elevators tilt the nose up or down. Moveable air foils roll the glider from side to side. The rudder is used to adjust the direction.

Hang Gliders and Microlights

Hang gliders look something like big kites. A thin, but strong, nylon wing is joined to a metal frame. The pilot hangs under it in a harness.

▲ A hang glider pilot gets ready for takeoff. The pilot is linked to the frame by a harness.

To fly a hang glider, a pilot runs off a steep hill or mountainside. After a few steps, the wing takes the pilot's weight, and then the machine is gliding.

The hang glider pilot's main control is a metal crossbar. Moving this raises or lowers the front of the wing, so the hang glider climbs or dives. The pilot can turn by leaning to either side.

▼ This swept-wing hang glider is a popular type. The pilot hangs below the wing.

metal frame

nylon wing

Microlights were first developed as hang gliders with engines.

    Many of today's machines are still like that. The microlight above has seats but is still controlled by a crossbar. Other microlights are really mini-planes, complete with a cabin and a front engine.

▲ A camera on the front of the wing gives a different view of this microlight.

► This microlight looks like an ordinary aircraft. It even has a cockpit.

Soft Wings

Paragliders look like parachutes but can be flown like a glider. They have a soft wing made of nylon fabric.

◀ Controlling a paraglider before takeoff can be difficult in gusty winds.

A paraglider is a glider in a bag. When it is unfolded and laid out, it lies flat on the ground, joined to a harness by a maze of cords.

To take off, a pilot faces into the wind and walks or jogs forward, with the cords and glider dragging behind. Then, air flows into holes (called "cells") at the front of the wing. Moments later, the fabric inflates into a wing shape that flies overhead.

cells at front of wing

◀ Light winds are best for safe flying. Landings should be smooth and gentle.

Grit your teeth and go!

Paragliding looks smooth and easy—and once you are off the ground it is really super. But leaping off a hill for the first time takes courage, even when you know the wing should keep you from falling.

Some training courses tow learners on a line, behind a truck, and this is not so scary!

When the wing is overhead, the pilot runs downhill and takes off. Two lines give steering control. To turn left, the pilot pulls the left line. The right line is pulled for right turns. Pulling both lines slows the paraglider for landing.

▲ Hilly places are good for paragliding. Updrafts allow for hours of flying.

Skydiving

Parachutes were invented to save flyers from being killed in air crashes. Today, sky divers jump out of aircraft just for fun!

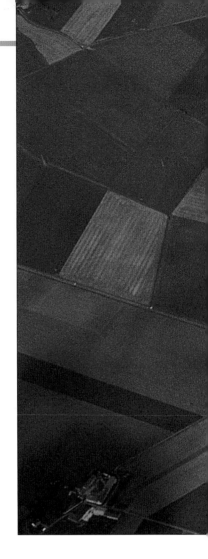

◀ A sky diver can use a board to do spins, rolls, and twirls on the way down. This is a sport called sky surfing.

feet strapped to board

Imagine this! You're in a noisy aircraft, leaning out of an open door. You look down, and there's *nothing* between you and the ground, 2 miles (3 km) down.

Then you jump, and seconds later you're falling fast. After a 30-second drop, you pull a handle. The parachute pops open, and you float gently to the ground. That's the thrill of skydiving!

High above the beach

Parascending at a seaside resort can give you a feel for parachuting without having to jump out of an aircraft. You're strapped to your parachute and towed into the air by a speedboat. In seconds you have a fantastic view!

▲ Sky divers link up to form a midair flower pattern. In a few seconds, they will let go and release their parachutes.

◄ A sky surfer starts a drop. One Swiss Air Force sky surfer uses a board shaped like his jet fighter!

▲ This plane performs at air shows. The windows under the wings help the pilot see out.

Spins, Rolls, and Loops

Aerobatics are the spins, rolls, and loops that an aircraft can perform in the hands of a trained pilot. These need great skill and lots of practice.

To perform aerobatics, a pilot needs good flying skills and a strong stomach. The movements of a plane rolling and twisting in the air are very violent!

Here's an example. When the plane does a loop, it pulls up into a climb, goes over on its back, and then roars down again into level flight.

▼ The Thunderbirds are a famous U.S. aerobatic team.

▶ Aerobatic teams are flown by top military pilots in fast jets. Here are the Red Arrows, flying a diamond-9 formation.

High-tech prop plane

This Russian Sukhoi is specially made for aerobatic displays.

It looks very old-fashioned, but it is packed full of the latest gear.

The wings are made of plastic and carbon-fiber—light but strong materials that are also used in Formula One racing cars.

The high-set bubble canopy gives the pilot a good all-around view while flying the plane.

canopy of clear plastic

powerful engine for good aerobatic performance

Old Planes

Though we are in the jet age, many people love old aircraft. A vintage plane can fly safely many years after it was made, if it is looked after properly.

▲ A 1930s Tiger Moth has only a few flight controls. Pilot and passenger can talk to each other, using a speaking tube. (See the arrow.)

Flying in an old aircraft is a reminder of the early days of flying. Only a stretch of grass is needed for takeoff and landing, instead of a concrete runway. The cockpit is open and the controls are simple. Instead of the roar of a jet, there's a spinning propeller.

▼ This Tiger Moth was used to train new pilots. It still performs rolls and loops, even though it was built more than 60 years ago!

▲ This wing-walking girl is a vital member of the flight team shown opposite.

In the 1920s, pilots called barnstormers thrilled people at air shows. Here are two of today's aces, flying with girls known as wing-walkers, who climb on the wing in flight. The girls use safety harnesses, but they still need nerves of steel for the show!

▶ Aircraft like these old Stearmans are called biplanes because they have two sets of wings. They fly slowly, so they are perfect for air shows.

wing-walker wears safety harness

Warplanes

Warplanes are planes that have flown in combat. Many warplanes were built to fight in World War II.

▲ The T-6 was first used as a trainer plane.

When they were made, many warbird planes were the fastest and deadliest machines in the air. Pilots flew them in combat—to kill or be killed. Today, warplanes are reminders of wartime's flying heroes. They are always the star attraction when they are flown at air shows.

▲ The P-40 was a fighter plane in World War II. This one is kept in flying condition by a special team.

► Looking after old engines takes time, care, and money. Here the Rolls-Royce engine of a Spitfire fighter plane is tested before a flight.

The canopy slides back to let pilot in and out.

wheels stored in wing during flight

Air Races

Pilots have raced planes
since the early days of flying.
Air races are still held today,
but the aircraft are much faster.

The earliest air races were held in 1909, at
the world's first air show, at Reims, in
France. In those days, aircraft flew much
slower. One pilot won a big prize for flying at
just 42 miles per hour (m/h) or (68 km/h).

The most exciting racing today is at
Reno, Nevada. Here aircraft fly at a low
level around tall towers that mark
the edge of the course.

Many of the racing planes are
warbirds, fitted with special engines. Top
speeds are nearly 500 m/h (800 km/h).

◀ The Gee Bees were racing
planes built in the 1930s.
One model was flown at
over 250 m/h (400 km/h)
in 1932, to set a world
speed record.

Racer built for speed

Here is one of the fastest Reno racers. It is based on a P-51D fighter plane, but it has a special engine, shorter wings, a tiny bubble canopy, and is bright red. In 2000, this plane won a prize for roaring along at 462 m/h (744 km/h).

*Bubble canopy gives
pilot a great view.*

▲ This Sea Fury plane is named *Miss Merced*. It was first used by the Canadian Navy in 1948. The plane has a new engine and can fly at almost 270 m/h (700 km/h).

New Ideas

You can buy a kit of parts to build this sleek Varieze plane in a garage.

New air equipment is always being made. Stronger fabrics may lead to better hang gliders and lightweight engines can use less fuel.

One way to go flying is to buy a kit of plane parts, and build your own plane. These aircraft are called home-builts. You only need basic craft skills to build them, but they take a long time to build properly.
It can take years to get a machine ready for flight.

In the future, home-builts may be easier to put together. Meanwhile, gliding and the soft-wing air sports are a much cheaper way to start flying.

◄ Paramotors were perfected in the 1990s. The pilot wears a small engine strapped to his back and flies along using a paraglider wing.

▲ The French Pétrel home-built can take off from land or water.

two-seat cockpit

▲ This is a design for a flying car. Lift fans would let it take off straight up from your front drive.

Could there be a flying car?

Maybe. Building a flying machine that can do the job is not too difficult. Making it as cheaply as a car is much harder. Also, learning to fly is more difficult than driving, so a flying car might have to be computer-controlled for safety.

Air Sport Facts

Here are some facts and stories from the world of air sports.

▲ This balloon flew to the North Pole in May 2000.

Around the world

In 1999, two balloonists flew the huge *Breitling Orbiter III* around the world, a distance of 26,602 miles (42,810 km).

The trip took just over 19 days, thanks to accurate weather forecasting and high-speed winds in the upper atmosphere.

Coldest balloon trip

In May 2000 another balloon, *Britannic Challenge*, reached the North Pole. There had been only one attempt before, in 1897.

The crew of that balloon died when they came down on the ice. Their bodies were not found until 33 years later.

Mega takeoff

In 1987 no less than 128 hot-air balloons took off in less than an hour, during a balloon festival in Britain. In April 2000, 20 Dutch skydivers jumped from a hot air balloon, the most to do so in one try.

Tiny planes

The *Baby Bird* is the smallest plane in the world. Built in 1984, the tiny single-seater has wings just 63 feet (1.91m) across, and is 11 feet (3.35m) long. It weighs only 374 pounds (114 kg) complete with engine, but can zoom along at nearly 112 m/h (180 km/h).

Going up!

The highest-ever glider flight was made in 1984 by U.S. pilot Robert Harris. He flew to a height of 49,010 feet (14,938m).

▲ The Britannic Challenge landed in the icy sea after the North Pole trip. The balloon was blown sideways for 30 minutes before stopping safely.

Long distance

Gliders can go long distances in the hands of experts. The record is held by pilot Klaus Ohlmann, who has flown for an amazing 1,530 miles (2463 km) in Argentina, South America.

BASE jumpers

Some people need even more thrills than skydiving can give. BASE stands for Buildings, Antennas, Spans, and Earth objects. BASE jumpers leap off such places as skyscrapers, TV masts, bridges, and cliffs.

These objects are much lower than a normal aircraft jump, so a BASE jumper usually has only a few seconds in which to open a parachute and land safely.

▶ This BASE jumper leaped off a tall pylon. He landed safely, but was he brave or just plain silly?

▶ The tiny Gee Bee Model Z was one of the fastest air racers of the 1930s.

Built in a garage

There is no official record for the quickest assembly of a home-built aircraft, but many of them take longer than you might think. One builder has been putting together a Varieze for 13 years, and it's still not ready to fly!

Longest flight

In 1986 Dick Rutan and Jeanna Yeager broke a record by flying their *Voyager* aircraft round the world nonstop. They covered 25,012 miles (40,252 km), flying at 116 m/h (187 km/h). They had less than 18 gallons (70 l) of fuel left in the tank when they landed!

The small parachute pulls the main parachute from backpack.

cockpit

monoplane wing

▲ The Gee Bee R-2 was an early monoplane design.

Air Sport Words

Here are some technical terms used in this book.

aerobatics
(air-uh-BAT-iks)
Controlled stunts carried out by a pilot to make an aircraft perform loops, rolls, spins, and other movements like dancing in the sky.

◀ This diagram is a plan for an aerobatic display. It is stuck in the plane's cockpit during the show.

airfoil
An airfoil is on the edge of a plane's wing.

BASE jump
(BAYSS JUHM-pur)
A low-level parachute jump from a building, an antenna, a span, or earth object (such as a cliff or mountain). Low-level parachute drops are always risky, so BASE jumping is outlawed in many places.

biplane (BYE-plane)
An aircraft with two sets of wings, one above the other. Early aircraft were mostly biplanes. Today, aircraft have a single-wing design, and are called monoplanes.

bubble roof (BUH-bul roof)
A one-piece clear covering that gives a pilot an all-around view.

carbon-fiber
(KAR-buhn FYE-bur)
A material in which thin shreds of carbon are mixed with a gluelike resin. When the mixture sets, it becomes stiff and strong—lighter than metal of the same size and shape.

cell (sel)
The name for open holes in the front of a paraglider wing and some parachutes. Air pushes into each cell, inflating the fabric to form a wing.

cockpit (KOK-pit)
The part of an aircraft where a pilot sits. In a large aircraft the cockpit is bigger and is usually called the flight deck.

flight controls
(FLITE kuhn-TROHL)
Controls that move parts of an

◀ A glider takes off, towed into the air by a winch cable.

winch cable

aircraft. Movable airfoils on the wings control roll. Elevators at the tail control climb and dive. The rudder adjusts direction.

glide (glide)
To move through the air without an engine. Gliders need rising air to stay in the air. Without lift, a glider pilot has to land soon.

lift (lift)
The upward force that wings give to an aircraft. Lift allows it to leave the ground. Glider pilots also use the word to describe any rising air.

microlight (MYE-kroh-LITE)
An aircraft weighing less than 660 lbs (300 kg-one seat) or

992 lbs (450 kg-two seats). They come in different designs, but have to keep inside these limits. They are also known as ultralights.

paramotor (PA-ruh-moh-ter)
A paraglider with a motor attached to the pilot's back.

parascend (PA-ruh-send)
To be towed into the air, behind a car or speedboat.

sky diver (SKYE-dye-vur)
Someone who falls for some time before releasing a parachute. A 9,850 ft (3000m) jump allows a drop time of about 30 seconds, before the parachute has to be released.

thermal (THUR-muhl)
A rising column or bubble of warm air. Glider pilots fly in tight circles inside thermals to climb high in the sky.

updraft (UHP-DRAFT)
An up-current of air that might be cold, if it is blowing up the side of a hill.

winch launch
(WINCH-LAWNCH)
A way of towing a glider into the sky. A long cable is run from a winch then hooked to a glider's nose. The cable is wound in fast, the glider is dragged forward, then takes off. The cable is dropped at about 2,000 ft (600m) up.

▼ A mechanic looks after an F-16 aerobatic jet.

Air Science

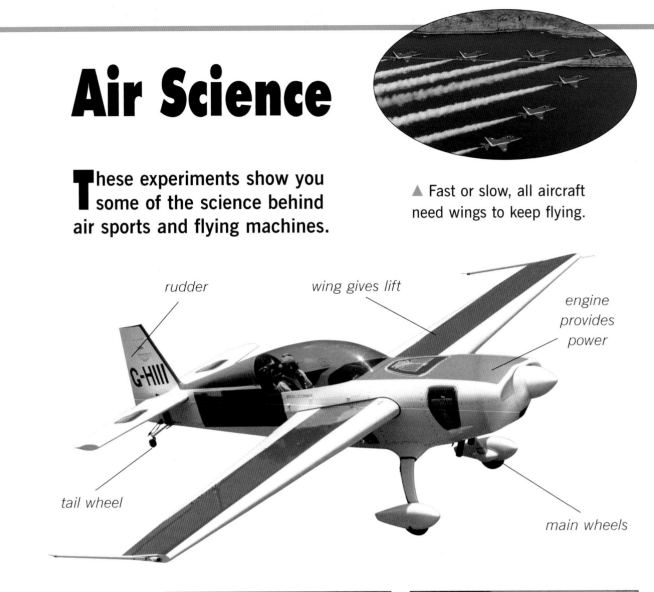

These experiments show you some of the science behind air sports and flying machines.

▲ Fast or slow, all aircraft need wings to keep flying.

rudder

wing gives lift

engine provides power

G-HIII

tail wheel

main wheels

How does a wing lift an aircraft?

As a plane moves forward, air flows over the wing's top quicker than under the wing.

This faster-moving air makes a low-pressure area. The wing is sucked upwards.

1 You need a thin sheet of paper and a drinking straw. Place the paper over the edge of a table.

2 Hold the straw close to the top of the paper and blow hard. The paper should lift up as you blow.

▶ This balloon is almost ready to fly. The ground crew are hanging on tight, ready to let go when the pilot gives the order.

How do balloons rise into the air?

Hot-air balloons work because hot air rises. The balloon's air is heated by a gas burner. The air still has weight, but it is lighter than the cooler air outside. So the balloon floats upward.

crew in basket, ready for takeoff

1 You need a sheet of tissue paper and a pair of scissors. Carefully cut out some tissue about 2.3 square inches (15 square cm). You now need some hot air. A warm radiator should give off enough heat.

2 The radiator's heat rises in an invisible column. Place the paper over the radiator to see it fluttering upward, too.

Index